RAINSHADOW EDITIONS

Garnet Moon. Paul Zarzyski. 1990.

Seven Nevada Poets. Ed. William L. Fox. 1991.

With Respect for Distance. Gailmarie Pahmeier. 1992.

Generous Journeys/Travesias Generosas. Marjorie Agosín. 1992.

Snowmelt. Shaun T. Griffin. 1994.

Geograph. William L. Fox. 1994.

Furniture Dreams. Marjorie Agosín. 1995.

Ride the Silence. Linda Hussa. 1995.

The Rings Around Saturn. Maria Theresa Maggi. 1996.

The Concept of Bodily Objects. Catherine Webster. 1997.

Bones Set Against the Drift. Bill Cowee. 1998.

And I You. Donna Hanelin. 1998.

And I You

Donna Hanelin

And I You

Illustrations by
Eva Jordan

Rainshadow Editions
The Black Rock Press
University of Nevada, Reno
1998

8.12.02
Oaxaca, Mexico
Deborah.
  Best wishes for your journey
into the world of writing! I look
forward to seeing your sense of play
and humor form into stories -- Enjoy,
          Donna

Printed in the United States of America

ISBN 1-891033-12-3

Rainshadow Editions
The Black Rock Press
University Library/322
University of Nevada, Reno
Reno, NV 89557-0044

Previous Appearances
"Paradise" and "Introduction to Fish." *Poems By Nobody.* June, 1993.
"And I You." *Wild Duck Review.* February-March, 1995.
"Song of Sixpence." *Poetry Now.* November, 1997.
"Birth Chant." *Poetry Now.* December, 1997.

ACKNOWLEDGMENTS

The author wishes to acknowledge the Poets Playhouse in Nevada City, California where these poems were first performed, 1992-1997. Many thanks to dear friend Su Rannells for listening and proofreading; to Mary K. Greer for magic of undying optimism; to my father, Joseph Hanelin, for his love and support. To Bob Blesse, thank you for everything, kindness included.

For illustrations and laughter, great love and gratitude to my daughter, Eva Jordan.

For my surrogate parents
Leo Tolstoy and Mother Goose

CONTENTS

AND I YOU

Say for me instinct means more than words
Ever will and I leave bed just long enough
To say so. Say for me poetry is gibberish
Something to do when no one is home.
And say for you it is something sacred—
The answer to a prayer. A gold chain to eternity.
Say one day we meet and I ask you
If you are well and you say yes but
Poems don't come and you ask me
If the poems come and I say yes but
I am not well and you envy me
The link to divinity
And I you a place on earth.

THEN THE BABY CRIED

I said to him
we can't play God
we can't kill people
and he said
there is no God
then I said the state becomes father
if the father can kill
the son can kill and he said
I guess it would be better
if we didn't kill at all.
But that wasn't the end of it
because I said we have to feel pain
there's no help for it
he said he didn't like it
he wasn't going to feel it again
I could if I wanted he said
damned if he would.
So you'd rather be sick than cry I asked.
Crying isn't pain he said
Crying is a release
Then the baby cried
And I had to leave the phone.

BIRTH CHANT

I was born, born over
over again like iron wheels
on the train as we went from Boston
to Detroit back home to Boston
as we flew as we fly as I
flew alone or together
or alone as I flow
with child as I flow as I fly
as I drove we drive I was born
I was born over I shed skin
as we flew as we drove quick
I was born I breathed sharp
I remember
I was born to my mother over
like iron wheels on the tracks
as we went from Boston to Detroit
we went as we go over, over
again into night mother
cried for perfection all was flawed
as we drove to Detroit watching wires
back again as I flew as I fly
we go prettily my big boys
on both sides the car spins her wheels
my life dizziness I was born
sterile air inhaled I do not
remember the cord coiled down
as we went as we go

dark cord curled I do not know
is it true? was she mother?
to her I look as we flew we fly
in a storm to Detroit I held
her hand my breath scent of death
as we flew in the clouds as we fly
plane strikes air lightning rivets
my mother she was as we flew here
we are all along as we go
I was born to a sigh of relief
home with child and we flew
we live we die we rise and I
was born to my child the cord
I remember curled dark and strong
she was born I remember red
baby curled on me and we flew
toddler paced up the aisle
to Boston to visit I was born
where she died there
lifelines I remember cool
and grey she was born as we flew
in the storm she was born
and she flew on the train flew
to the night flew through the storm
to the arms of her mother who
was born who remembers
the cord who was born
who has died who flew in the train
who made visits to a child whose child
flew I was born I remember
my child she was born and we fly
with the moon through a storm.

WHAT WE CAN NOT CHOOSE

In the dark city night
Where men with nothing else
Pass in and out of gated halls
I hold my daughter close
Rush past pending danger
Inject her with my fright.
I had hoped to give just love, boundless
Instead, I gave everything.

OPEN DOOR

It happened to my Mother
The joke you hear all the time
Great operation, the patient died
So her parting experience
At the hand of the heart surgeon
I never met him
It was all I could do to keep
Both legs under me
Never took valium since.

My Mother spoke of death twice
Once ten years earlier after the Surgeon General
Told us to quit smoking
I'll live 'til I die
Stubborn and stupid as anyone around
She said it
I didn't know when she died
I would have no mother
You selfish shit I would have said
Leaving me here alone
With three men.
We were all there before surgery
Cheerfulness as stifling as the air inside
I'll see you after I said
I don't think I'll make it she said
And that was the second time
She mentioned death

Sure you will I said
Having no idea it would be possible
To live without a mother.
What I said up there about valium
Wasn't true.
Before the funeral I took it again
Felt it blanket me in the back of the black
Limousine as I gripped the hands next to me
Knowing I had the most to lose.
'Yea though I walk through the valley
Of the shadow of death I shall fear
No evil'— a poster like a set
Backdrop for a casket. Nothing real
My Mother's sisters. Nothing real
My Mother's shell, the dead body
I refused a last look. Nothing real

If you have had no idea of the spirit
You will get more than an inkling
When your Mother dies
You will see the birds fly, you will know spirit
Same as you have known flesh
It rushes in through the open door
It doesn't leave, it grows and becomes life
Where there was a stone cold heart the blood flows again
The love of the birdsong blood red at scarlet sunrise
When you think you can no longer live.

Fifteen years later
I danced at the home of a heart surgeon
Ritual dance of life

Private birthday for Mom
Private and final separation from spouse
Things come in threes: private prayer
For all children that we will live
    and make peace.
But I hate the heart surgeon
I hate her stuffed animals, ex-pets embalmed
I hate her lovely home
I hate the collected stuff of truth
I like her dignity my friend says
But I am quiet and wonder
What the hell he's talking about.
I hate the ritual.

I love the dance
I love the woman who lets me pretend
    she's his next wife
I love the running and rolling of my hips
I love the drumbeat that stays the same and
    sounds different all the time
I love the cat that sounds like the bird in refrigerators
I hear the rattle that sounds like the snake
The view is breathtaking
I walk diagonal across the spiral
I have never stayed on track
I watch the leader breathe heavy over women
And head back to the spiral
Soon I love everyone.

Bob I said it would be like taking my Mother
If I had taken my Mother when she died
And stuffed her and kept her on the rocking chair.

It's OK he says, he wants to be stuffed.
For me I say ashes to ashes dust to dust.

Five days later
I dreamt there was a woman in terrible pain
After heart surgery
I dreamt her body and face writhing
On a hospital bed next to my hospital bed
Pain so great I woke up
A nightmare unlike any other:
No strange beasts or strong men chasing me
No choking from food that won't swallow
No hands floating in space
No huge black spiders in slow motion toward me
No rubbery bugs standing up fighting with swords
No thefts, no murders, no rapes
No fires, no winds, no floods
No giant waves rising
No snow
No cliffs
No closed rooms
No snarling dogs
Teeth are all in place
I am wearing my own clothes
I remember the lines
There is no stage
The lovers don't leave
Friends don't turn their backs
My brothers love me
The figures have heads   and bodies.

A nightmare unlike any other:
My Mother after surgery
No heart, only pain.
Lived 'til she died
Just like she said
Stupid and stubborn as anyone ever
Was.

FINISHED CLEANING UP

The morning after Mom
Was put in a box and buried
So she couldn't clean up after
The after the funeral party
I figured the food was bad.

One hand on the switch
One on the pastrami
Dry-eyed
I stood lost in the rumbling grind
Just watching the meat
Go down the drain.

SO GLAD I BROUGHT ALONG
MY HANKIE

Five dead moths turning on green scum
Shallow waters, under cedars
Five dead moths swirling on emerald water
Fallen petals, pale and brittle
Caught in a whirlpool.
I cry for five dead moths
Stuck in a swirl.
I dry my eyes. White flower petals
On emerald waters, under cedars
Steady in their circle.

SQUIRREL

The squirrel fit in your palm
bloody nose, eyes closed
near dead on the forest floor
(You should not touch it,
disease and contamination)
You held it in your right hand
as if human heat were magic
and made your left the lid
the way any child would
who once had a mother
Back home you traded your warmth
for a pink terry towel
washed blood off with a tiny white rag,
something you made judging size
of your nose, tissue, its nose
You dropped water in its mouth
and saw the welcome swallow
(You should not touch.
It's nothing but a tree rat
don't let that cute tail fool you.)
But alive, it's alive
Did you frighten it?

* * *

If it wasn't for that silvery look in his eyes
(you admit men are a weakness)
you would never have listened
when he said yes, of course

there are aliens
yes, they experiment on us
and they do know everything
Yes, they are what we name God,
we are just baby squirrels he said
in their weird hands.
They don't even have to read our thoughts
they know us as if they are us.
We're simple like your calico cat
lying half baked in the window light
or simpler like your little dog
barking at the shadow of a circling hawk.
Why even pretend
you are in control of your life?
But what were you supposed to do
chalk it all up right then
donate your time on earth
to the mind warp of a phantasm?
You told the squirrel:
I assure you I am not an alien
I am human and want to save your life
When I wipe the blood from your nose
Fold inside cloth the bit of trembling fur you are
I know what it is to take care
like any child would
who once had a mother, oh, but mother
why even pretend you're in control?

* * *

You put the towel burrito of squirrel
on the passenger seat, drive to the vet
in what is now a driving rain—

that squirrel would have been dead
if it wasn't for you.
(You shouldn't touch it, a warm spot
of swarming lice and bad blood.)
Maybe you don't have control of life
but in this moment there's no time
to ponder, you just try.
(Why, to keep another rabid squirrel
in our North American woods?)
Yes they know you, he said, the type
who reverts to the rescue of riff-raff
disregards the serious dealings of death:
famine, frost, war, flood, fatigue,
disease, decripitude, and slow but sure mass suicide.
You take no stand for or against anything,
you're just a dumb busty ape
sentimental for a puny heartbeat
stuck inside anything warm. They know you.
(Don't touch the baby,
the mama will abandon him,
better to leave him for dead.)

* * *

Once the aliens get you he said
you'll never fit in again
(as if I was fitting in now you thought)
you'll know what no one else knows
no one believes you.
people just fall apart.
Then he told you (damn those eyes),
everything for him happened in a group

Everything? you wondered, you said nothing
ever happened for you in a group
hardly even in threes or twos.
He offered to teach you how to pray
(you know who taught him)
What's the use you asked
if they take my words away?

* * *

The vets salivate over your squirrel,
they argue who will hold her and they do say *her*
after pulling the tail up vertical
while fluorescent lights shudder the room
the voices near thunder
as they poke her and probe her—
all this for a lone babe
who could have died peacefully
in the pine needles by the stream
and you wonder why, why didn't you
just let it sleep there in a point of shade
covered by sound of ripple and rain,
bird calls, bird songs and bug and frog,
why didn't you just leave that scrap alone
sweetly losing breath into the forest,
why did you grab it up greedy for a pulse,
for gratitude, for pride of lives saved,
savage to know everything
to experiment and to control.
(I'll teach you how to pray he said
alone downstairs he spent hours
on his knees and I thanked God.)

What they do they told you
is give her to a volunteer feeder.
When she can chomp acorns on her own
they reinstall her where you found her,
she'll find her old family,
take up residence again
in the hole they call home.
But will she ever fit in again you ask—
oh yes she'll lead a happy life
they assure you
and as you head out the glass double doors
they call you back to the counter
and hand over your pink terry towel.

CALL HOME

My daughter calls distressed
At the advent of virtual reality
In the city where she lives she says
There are people who never remove their shoes.
She sees now why I choose these unadvanced woods
Reality refused by the refined
The accusation humming: I live in a dream.
I hid my tears from you I told her
When we went to the mountains and you were small
I cried for the peaks and the valleys
She does it too she says sitting in the ocean sand
She cries for the fury of the shoreline
Hidden in this godless, almost real world.

THOUGHTS AS THE DEATH
OF L.J. APPROACHES

Lead me please
When I am dying
Into the woods to sleep
Under the oaks and pines
I am not afraid of the weather
And delight at my dead flesh
Eaten by vulture, crow and worm.
For the last time to breathe the air
To see the branch broken sky
The first wild flowers of Spring
To feel the mushrooms push
Against my sallow worn out skin.
The neighbor dogs are welcome
To a sniff with snouts
Raised for the curious as they hear
The birds sing—one, my Mother
As she waits for me
To make her nest again.

SQUID

The squid stretches one arm up onto the boat
and grabs a boy for dinner
Before the first bite the boy looks at the squid
and sees someone kind like Uncle Harry
with ocean water dripping from his round brown eyes
The boy has time to think maybe Uncle Harry is crying
at having to eat his nephew, quite this young
but it's too late, instinct takes over
The boy is bit and digested into a tidy little mass
The squid is content except
for certain indigestible ornaments, a toy revolver, a belt buckle.
Twinge of regret.
Eight days later hungry
The squid scoots under the boat again
Stretches up for a lunch of sweet leg of boy
Only this time the men are ready—
They hack off the arm and another and another
Then head home to unload the ten suckered snakes.
Women squeal to the men in welcome
and squirm at the tangled trophies. They slice and beat them
and roast them for the feast—a funeral party for the lost son
And for one other—
For Uncle Harry down at the bottom,
For armless Uncle Harry rotting at the bottom of the sea,
For dear Uncle Harry's eyes still staring up
    from the sandy bottom of the sea.

INTRODUCTION TO FISH

When the water men drain
the ditch of water
the fish are left belly up
I cry and fling them
into the woods

I asked the Chinese man
if the fish in the tank
would be food
No, no this is carp
cost eight hundred dollars

Tiny squid swam in ginger sauce
at the bottom of the bowl
who knows what else we ate

A gorgeous feathery fish swam
at the Chinese restaurant
when we stood to leave
it was gone

Childhood goldfish
die one after another
I cry and flush them

WARNING

A white man threw a snowball at an Indian
The Indian was bleeding from his right ear
The Indian had seen the crocodile in the water
Then the mother with blue-eyed baby saw the crocodile
And no one believed her
Then a child rang the bell, the crocodile alarm
No one believed him either
This was in Florida
And there was a crocodile in the water.

WE RUN RAGGED

Carried on the backs of bees
I was squeezed into the fluttery hive
A wax coffin confounded by the drip of honey
Slow and steady as I died to the drone song
The machine dirge, the north wind
Relentless in my see-through room
Bees bottoms scrambling to their places
Among the six-sided cells, the Utah desert of conformity
An instinct prison.
We rail against the symmetrical
Beg for something beyond a cube
We take egg beaters to the great salt seas
Searching for a new shape under the sun.
We run ragged, the creative.
In wax coffin dying the death
Of no breath and fear of the sting
I search for something small square and bland
I pray the six sides, my sixth sense, the edible coffin
The dazzling snowflakes—I pray all would leave me be.

When my father raved I always ran
To the bathroom to quiver behind a locked door
Stared there at the six-sided tiles
Transfixed at the sure tight fit.
When the sounds outside died
I went headdown quiet to the attic
Where I examined the jewels my brothers
Stored in the old round tall stove

Where my baby doll waited for me
With her beautiful blank stare of enduring love
Where tiger lay for me to fix
Small pleasures on his stuffed tail
Where I would forget the foment below
Where the king bee flew random, stinger out,
To pain and scare whatever came his way.

When it snows here in the Sierra
The flakes don't show up the way they did
On my red wool mittens in Natick
Where I stood knee deep in snow
Staring at my palm until the cold itched.
Did the snow give me passage to the tile?
Was the coffin, the journey with the bees
A long first lesson in the sixth sense?
Was tiger named Six?
The birth day is a six.
Is there a curse here of memory
Or am I graced with detail?
Is tile grout something mystical—
If so, why does it turn black
Unless ungodly diligence is paid?

FOREFATHERS

Cheerful four days since I dreamt
My true relation to Count Leo Tolstoy
Since I told my family of the love affair
which produced my great great grandmother,
Passionate love of old Pappy Tolstoy
for a tall Jewish serf.
My family, when I told them, reacted
Strangely which they often do:
Dad kept talking about there being no doctors
in Oregon and California
Others passed eyes back and forth,
compact jellied eyes hand-to-hand
popping them in and out, a dance from the undersea.
Dad kept saying we had to be doctors but I,
I felt better than I had in years
Inside clear dreams of my Tolstoyan ancestry.

PEACE

It is pleasant to pretend my child
Is full of good will toward me
    In this season of peace
Yet she is simply a self striving
    To be itself
And I am babbling jetsam on her sea.

SONG OF SIXPENCE

Counting beats to the word   words in a line   lines to a poem counting
Camels   miles to the cottage   counting chromosomes
Counting dots on a die   counting my downs   counting
Hugs 'n kisses counting inconveniences   counting your ups
Counting degrees of heat   courses in a degree   degrees of cold
Counting holes in our shoes   counting knots of wind   counting
Teeth left in your mouth   counting the dreary
Counting tin cans   counting the sick
Counting ships at sea   lost socks   specks of dust on the shelf
Counting the starving   counting years 'til I die   counting
Dried dishes   your downs   hairs on my legs   counting
Square yards of vacuumed shag
Counting feet of picket fence   counting hours asleep counting
My ups   counting days since we met
Counting seconds of breath held crossing bridges
Counting chickens   counting eggs: twelve   counting leg lifts
Counting days 'til you die   counting brown pennies
The King was in his counting house   counting out his money
Counting strikes: three   counting past lives counting
T-cells   minutes of hysteria   murders premeditated
Counting brain waves   heartbeats   Are you alive now?
Counting the dead, the weary, the wicked   counting plastic jugs
Counting pounds of the body   years of famine: seven   counting
Debt, gross national   counting trees downed in the jungle counting
Board feet   counting who takes the kids for how long
Counting debt, gross private   months since intimacy   the troops
Counting dead blades of grass   counting how many other men

Counting time in   atoms   counting destructive ability   counting
Time out   counting blackbirds in a pie   fleas in the fur
Counting inches of snow   counting number of drinks before driving
Counting you looked so many minutes at how many other women?
Counting visits to your mother   counting nights you go alone
Miles of fault   counting generations until extinction
Counting spiders in the shower   counting brothers
Visits to my father   counting years ago we stopped talking
Counting how much each mistake costs deducting it from a salary
Mythical   counting cubic yards of waste   counting sperm
Counting pelts   counting years of feast: seven   counting
Raspberries in the basket   pups in the litter   counting
Wonders of the world   counting black seeds in a melon
Counting breath in....four   counting breath out........eight
Counting minutes between contractions   yards of red silk
Counting years to freedom   seconds to transformation
Counting newborn fingers   counting newborn toes
The Queen was in the parlor   eating bread and honey

I AM THE QUEEN NOW

As jewels, as velvet, as the deep carpets lay before my feet,
As the king speaks, or the sea lions roar, as honey
   and the modern earth
As light years, light skies and the light in your eyes
When the candle wick quits
As you wake as slow as the mountains and hot
There is the queen, believing.
My kingdom, my kingdom, my queen's domain
My spark unconquerable carried so close within
None can take the throne, or the land, or the treasures.
You may read in the queen's library
A room of daily life, of the scrapes of baby queens,
The diet of young kings, the need for clothing, for a roof,
For the order of the house, for the timely talks of the events
Of other people's lives,
A library of the courage it takes to wake.
Yawning, yawning in the queen's presence?
You want a medal for getting out of bed?
A golden sword for drinking your tea by nine?
A carriage and horses because you dressed before noon?
You want a palace of your own for writing
A thank you note to your Aunt Dora back in Detroit?
You may have them all
I am the queen now and you are my best friend.

My daughter's father is in the hospital
Trouble in the guts again
It's not my fault this time—
Fifteen years since we made the same bed

We talked two hours today why
Did I dwell in the past?
He is my daughter's father. Nothing changes that.
And because I needed to know
I could sit in a hospital room unafraid.
Unreasonable you say facing mortality
Unreasonable to have no fears
Unreasonable to be calm in the face of pain?
I am the queen now. Queens die.
Kings die.
We all die in our own royal time.
Who is the body who holds the voice who calls for calm
    in the face of death?
Grandpa when he was very old said don't talk to me
About death or the pogroms in Russia.
Look at the strudel Grandma baked, have some chicken
Later we'll go for a walk, the two of us,
To the train tracks and watch the 6:43 roll by.
Dad, when he was the age I am now, said
Ninety percent of illness is psychosomatic
Don't go to a doctor unless you're dying.
I have come to believe we get better or we get worse
When we get worse there might be help for it
Just don't talk to me about death or the victims of rape.

My daughter's father asked
Will you marry again?
Never I said
Are you afraid of being sick and alone?
No I am not afraid
Can I spend my life afraid?

I have already wasted ten years afraid
To enter the hospital room
I'm asking he said because I just turned forty
Sick in the hospital.
The queen is tired
Morning enters on the telephone screaming
Winged serpents twisting fiery
Bringing bringing great fury
When they stop to speak they say nothing
That couldn't wait for afternoon.
Remember what I told you before dear?
I don't know if it's true
I don't know if anything is true
If I am true or he is true
Or the serpents, are they true?
Do the mountains carry true?
Does the phone ring true?
Is sleep needed?
Is love?

My dear friend, I love you same as before
You are the one I talk true to
You are the spark inside the night's fall
Winter's winter fire storms up chimneys and out into the dark air
You are the moment I return to and the warmth off my skin
You are the instant between heartbeats
When I am dead and alive at once.
You are the words
I am the queen
You are near to me
Believing.

TO BE

I am who I am
I fall in love as I do
I get angry as I will
I cry as I have
I laugh when I can
To be I write
A simple life
Few deceptions
Daily exercise
Ordinary machines break
Pleasures are cheap
Anxieties limited
Health intact
In the rain
I wear my boots
That's a change

JUSTIFICATION

Why am I so tired after writing?
How can I justify this lazy life
On my ass, no strain in my hand?
Try it,
Fluttering between two worlds.

Red woodpecker walks backwards
On the underside of a tree limb
Poking diligently at the sustenance
Above him
If he had to try for it
He would beg for a sweet nest
Lined with fur and feather
He would be tired also.

DEAR SPECK

There is an ancient loneliness
Holds me by the tree
It is unforgiving like death
Knows no solutions
like life itself
I fight the distant message
Ward off the stark
Confuse my own being
with the condition of being
Pride forces me to strive
for the fine and ideal friend
Trees know
And motion when I pass
Sadness is not within you
It is without you and throughout
If we had eyes we'd weep
Water down to deepest roots.
Let your leaves fall
Lie naked in the winter
Stand tall green in summer
On fire in bright yellow autumn—
If we had five fingered hands
We'd keep the leaves from falling
Sadness is not within you.
There is an ancient loneliness
Holds me by the tree

Artists paint it
Poets write it
As if of our selves.
The self is a speck.
Fly with the wind dear speck
Float in the rain
Glide on the ice
Bump along on the summer breeze
Dear Speck.

SUBMARINE

Moments of my life do not disturb me
It's the glue in my veins slowing me down
(In dilution I lead an easier life)
Events make no difference
Only internal solutions
Events make no difference? Then why
Do you respond to each word spoken
Every speaker, to the twilight, to a look
To a motion, a mention, a glimpse, a flitter
  like milkweed seed on a breeze?
I try to be part of the world
No time for your fairy stories
    and all this blowing in the wind
I can not get out of bed as nothing more than a speck
    mad with the changes around me
I need strong bones inside muscle nerve blood
Prime mammal—a solid piece of life
    certain of my hold on this earth
No more of this speck stuff when I begin to run
I have to know it's my own beloved strength
    not the north wind sweeping me from behind
Okay—don't be so sensitive
Don't get depressed   don't look so sad
Keep smiling kid keep smiling
  you look great when you smile
Up with friends   (how 'bout a counselor
how 'bout a drug   how 'bout a new car
how 'bout a submarine)

Sure I'll take the submarine—
We'll go on a secret mission down
Down to visit the fish of the night
Fish with gross tentacles, see-through skin
    and ever yawning jaws
We can pay them for an hour or two
To lie in their depths, to fuck with our unknowns
To seduce the secret of phosphorescence
To discover how internal solutions
Illuminate those basement shores
Here is the sub as you requested
Take a deep breath and climb on in
Friend, I was talking metaphor
No, you don't want metaphor
You want bone and blood
You want the body to know
Where it is. You want your feet
Resting firm on the floor
Open the hatch I'm coming
Down into the part night
Through into the dark night
Lower and lower until the world
Glows from an inner light
Where all things contain themselves
In a calm almost too close to death
Where each creature holds itself
Shines its own light
Makes a beacon for no other
No divine path of slanted sunlight
Where the orchestra opens up full sound
Sending empty faced angels into the ozone.

In this silent dark of swimming light, you
Fish, hey, you fish
Do you hear anything?
Can you answer my prayer?
Do you ever stumble at the curb?
Do you goof?

My friend and I spent a day
   which was more a night
Cooped up in the sub
    with two small windows to watch
Fish at the bottom of the sea.
This was no picnic
next time I choose the new car
     and head off into a Sierran meadow
     with basket full of chicken and pickles
We can only tell you this
Fish have secrets we will never know
All we understand as desirable here
Means nothing there—there
Where the sky has no stars—no stars
And there is no sky at all

THE GREAT WAR

In the great war between
                        The right side of us
            and
  The left side of us
            There may come a time
                        When the weapons are put aside
            When we have
Killed the dead   So many times
            What's left?
Rubber duck   Flung over the shoulder
            Comedy

  Whosoever has one bright light left
                        Shines it to attract
        The Last Lone Warrior
            In the great war
                        Between the right side of us
            and
  The left side of us   We may at last
  Bump into that dear piece of us
            A Bridge
  To walk from left   to right
            and back again

          Freely

            No walls armed guards barbed wire outstretched

Claws

When we do   the cry for joy is silent

When I was sixteen and freshly raped
My brother told me
You have to love yourself first
Only then can you love
Someone else

PRAIRIE SONG

My stomach in knots from the summer's first
Potato salad or is it more from...
(Listen, Friend, I want to talk to you
I don't know where to begin)
I feel like I've been run over by a covered wagon
Slowly with two great thuds preceded by hoof kicks
Several tips of the whip from the sides.
They all say *protect yourself*
I tried, knotted my calves for the occasion
It wasn't enough.

They have machines now
To teach you how to acquire invisible iron arms
They have machines now for everything
It's the end of the Twentieth Century.
'So why not use the machines?'
You have to have money to buy them, I'm broke
The money rolled out of my pockets
Out there in Oklahoma lying on the prairie
      when the covered wagon hit
They won't hire me; they don't like bruises
      and gashes and limps
I'm not a pretty sight.
'Why not a machine to cover you up?'
You don't understand
What they do now
Is fill the workplace with machines
Beside each machine they put a beautiful woman
Or the shell of one, a sort of robot queen to push the buttons
On the machine and say *hello* as a human would.

The men are trained now to be excited by long red fingernails
But not so excited that they in any way show
Their excitement. The men are so well trained now
They work almost as well as the machines
(Am I afraid? Yes, Dear, I'm afraid
I'm scared to death of the machines
And the robot queens
And the well trained men
And the dirty work of trying
To be human.)

'Why don't you tell me what happened?'
Oh, you mean out on the prairie, it was a hot day
Prairie grasses were dry
I was walking along sweaty and proud
Watching the great blue sky and the space in front of me unchanging
My thoughts were roaring and crashing inside
Wondering as I did about the Twenty-first Century
       and life beyond the grave
About a gentle man I know, the touch of warm hands, good poetry
Proceeding into castles, kings and fleshy queens
Occasionally dipping into the storehouse of guilt: stealing
Quarters from my Mother, when mid-Twentieth Century
       a quarter bought five candy bars
And all the other bad things I did when no one knew and thought
I was good, then thinking back to sickness, death, handsome men,
       wealth, success, adventure and new towels for the kitchen
       maybe striped this time
So I did not hear the wagon approaching
Until it was on top of me when I saw the hooves of the horses

Rolled on my back too late—I was hit in the jaw—then the wheels
Up the side of me and over and back down. I tried to get up
The rear wheel came up over the front of me, across my stomach
Back down, blood everywhere, broken bones and
                    Visions of wagon trains backed up to the Mississippi.

It feels just great to talk to you
I haven't told anyone about this.
'Can you tell me more?'
The sun went down, a cool breeze moved the grass
The prairie dogs began party arrangements. I could hear them
Chattering, making food, decorating, sweeping out the sand.
I got it into my head that if I moaned straight down
Into the ground they would hear. I fell asleep,
When I woke there was no blood, only hairy green leaves
Covered my body and branches with a sweet bark encircled me,
A small water hole lined with leaves let me drink
                    one fingerful at a time.
I passed into sleep over and over again yet each time I woke
Fresh hairy leaves shaded and blanketed me.
The moon had turned full before I could move,
The gashes healed, my bones felt whole
I ate the bits of food now left by my water cup
I listened to the prairie dogs sweeping and burrowing.
(Dear Friend, when I slept I dreamt it was you
Tending me. I loved you more than ever for giving me life.)

When I walk now
I don't think so much
About the Twenty-first Century
Or life beyond the grave
I keep glancing around behind me
To make sure there are no blind machines
Strolling on the prairie.

MEN TALK EVIL AND GOOD

My men say there is evil in the world
But in time when I am long since dead
Desert sands grow pink, green and yield
Heaven will enter earth, good
Will hold the balance.
I only hope the well waves of good
Crest and fall in rhythm to my hips
Lest truth come as a rumble and leave
As lightning jagged in pained tree joints
Knees and elbows branching through the night.
    Let the voice of the men rise cool and low
      Against the narrow canyon of a woman's
        warm staccato wail

My men say there is evil in the world
But in time when I am long since dead
Frozen poles grow deep, leafed and yield
Heaven will enter earth, panic
Will stampede no action.
Yes, dear, there is evil in the world
But fear will not go on patterning human figures
In a two step line dance of terror
Scattered clunk of boot on wood, palm slapped
To denim buttocks extended
Flirting on demand with no consequence.

Men tell me there is evil in the world
But they will mount bright steeds in winter frost
They will ride in light to conquer it

They will ride through night to conquer it
They will ride dawn and dusk alike to conquer it
   Let the voice of the men rise cool and low
   Against the narrow canyon of a woman's
         warm staccato wail

When my men mount the pedestal
I only hope their voices hold
My shoulders open flat against the sheet
To show my heart typing at a faster rate
Hair pulled aside to make room for a mouth
Uttering truth after truth into a body
   made feeble by fears
Legs spread wide to bring the idea to fruit
Stretched and courting the next millennium.
   Let the voice of the men rise cool and low

TO BE A MAN

When I stop to cry
The burning tears for babies I never born
Thank the one I have for the experience
When I can see anger out the door
An invited guest to rouse me up
When the house is empty, no one left around
Comes my pity for men who never felt
Another life inside: the cold, bleak life
Always separate, always strong.

To be a man what hell, what relief
To never feel your own blood flow
Through another.
The blood gone, crying out for it to return
To never feel another heart beat inside of you
Heart long gone away from you
To be a man, what divine independence
To leave the family behind
To never go looking again for your own heart
While advising women to let go, to leave them alone
When this is leaving your own heart on the roadside.
What you've missed, what ice might form inside
To feel so strong, apart, and sure.

Men ought to go to war and fight
Work, build houses, protect the weak who must watch
Their own hearts slow beat far down the path.

Women must watch their strength—the double
Heartbeat—the overflow of blood—women must watch
And lie in arms. Women must let men hold them
And feel the blood pound against an angry shore.

ROCK-A-BYE BABY

Fear like bugshells suspended for years
Web and wing cling to the window, shiver in a breeze
Malignant ravings trap men; I hear
Glass slivers raining down the night sky
Screams rising, spiraling up and over
So sound and shake kept off sure smell of death
Inside the dining room
Fish stink the house on a warm afternoon
Groins lubricated in time for silica meteor showers,
Falling star, frantic spider barricades door
Weaves lovers in   locked   bound   sucked dry
Snow white skeletons shifting on the telephone lines
As voices from around town play these bones
Same as the bluegrass man played and clogged
Clean as a whistle, not a wrinkle, stared straight
Lifeless and talented we had to say
Because one has to say something about all this song and dance.
Men I hear get trapped. Spider transmogrifies—
Two legs become the swimmer, two the artist
Two a woman with the serene brown eyes of a cow
Two—breasts pushing purple spandex—topography for a double mound.
Larger than life limbs cross the floor
In a cha cha cha fiesta of divinity
Stopping inches from him to deliver one overlong look.
Men get trapped.

You laze in the web, an imported hammock and picture
Dad in the summer swaying after a long day and hot commute

Joint in hand, mind lolling in easy clarity which dissipates
Who where what when oh you? Sound waves vibrating your innards
Voices—an indigestion from the past.
You rock like the baby on the treetop
She weaves. You lie stoned dumb, rock blind
Deaf as pebbles beaten down by the waves
No legs now, no fiber of your own, you take hers,
Tingle in the web and fall into complexes
Same as the maple seed spins syncopated
Feeling for fertile ground—
Little hope here on the asphalt plot.

Curtains never go down, scene after scene
This death show is for you
Mom plays too she's moaning pain she needs you
Spider spins wraps cajoles and swears
Mom moans simpers begs and smiles
She uses your blood same as you once used hers
Now unnatural bond of man to earth you hold
Her naked body against your naked body
And imagine you are still Mom's child.
Yes, she has seen you like this.
Spider spins and binds
Sending hypersensitive web threads blocks long
To catch as catch can any new buzz in the wind
Death streams in the light of your windows
Captured and held in wood.
You sway and sink numb she punctures
Your eye and robs the mind from your mind
The blood and beat from your heart.

You think no one knows
But there is your sense somewhere far and muffled
A man inside a man, tears making a dank palace in your cave
Where one cub whimpers in the dark
A distressed tune for a spider traversing underwater
In an eight-legged polka around her poisoned mate.
Web and wing cling to your window, dear
Shiver in a breeze.

THIS CRITIC IS MALE

When I turn my back you are there
Ready to rip my heart from my head
To make maggot camps of my guts
Hiding a black pistol in the flowers
Lilac wafting, gun indents on my spine
You all set to release the paralyzing shot.
As I turn to meet my lover open to embrace
I feel the chill Ha of your reptile lungs
Exhaled down between our chests.
Dancing in a crowd in the surety of my own body
Braced up between drumbeats   tick in a whirl
You force a wedge through my pattern
Toes of lead nip at my ankles
Falter the dance newborn to my toes.
When I sit as I do today face to a poem
Lifetime trance of thought in spiral motion
I hear your morbid inhalation
Strengthening to suck away these words
I use for breath.

SOMETIMES THE TERROR IS FEMALE

I. She Tells Her Friend

It happened like this   through the darkness
His mother moaned from a hospital bed
I was in his bed   the other woman
Returned rapping on the glass at midnight
When he opened the door she struck his neck
He screamed boy-screams up the hill of dry grass
and back in bed he worried she'd burn the house.
I did not sleep very well that night
What with Mom and imminent flame
Nor did I sleep well last night as I dreamt again
of him and of her and of what vehicle delivered me
to that address and of what conveyance so kindly
Brought me home.

II. At the Same Time Other Strange Things Occur

Old man in masquerade brought forth a grandson with my name
Other I had loved became a wisp of cirrus near the sun
I feared my own strength, sank as seed into the avocado
      green secure and fit
I bound the bundle of straw tight and strong to balance
on my back down the steep slope
I hesitate to descend where in a hollow
masked man in orange fed yellow apples to dappled horses
Where in mad glee to overbig horse teeth
He passed fruit to feel sloppy tongues savor his fingers.

I fell in love with a donkey tethered to a parking meter:
I surveyed the street for long ears' other lovers
Seeing none I leaned toward his lips
He, more ardent, held my shirt in his teeth   our eyes
Met 'til startled by a revving engine
He let go of me and now this great love has also passed.
Oh, but to see again those two inch eyelashes, if even in a dream!
Raps on glass at midnight set teeth to grind
Sick mother burrows in a bent bed
Godawful woman glares words in right ear
Man's neck bursts to the strain
Sends boy-screams up dry night air
New found love gone

III. Other Woman Appears Again, Larger

Mama I hear thunder the little boy cries
Shut up now, boys don't cry. You see Papa crying?
But Mama a storm is coming, my kitty will drown
What's wrong with you a tough boy like you fussing over a cat
    Look out that window, do you see a storm?
No Mama it's sunny it's sunny now but I hear the thunder

She blackens the rising sun   casts shadow from Oklahoma
Across the Great Plains   lumbers west
Into the darkness of her own form
She scatters our prairie dogs   makes carpet of the corncobs
Noxious green steam of her breath felling bumblebee and ladybug
In her right hand she wields a weapon I once could name
But have long since buried same as my mother

In a quiet plot far far away   She storms
Mountains valleys plains always to the offbeat of hand
Slapped into resonant flesh of leg, left arm repelling her own thigh
In pendulous counterbalance on this awkward march

IV. She Arrives at the Shore

As her body falls to the sand of the California coast
Earth, a good mattress, ripples and groans to hold the weight
Still she grumbles and turns in a deserved sleep of shame
Misdeeds gathered inside   years of lashing others in
Uncountable epistles of blame   nothing held to self
Waking at noon she leans on the Coastal Range
To catapult herself upright   cools her toes in the Pacific
Blue crabs sidestep toward lighter ground
Fish schools shimmer and split half north half south
Sea lettuce drifts in a cellular search for the missing sun

I resent you she said to me when she was smaller
I resent you getting into his bed
I said nothing only stared into the future I knew must come
And as today examined the crest and fall of her mighty waves

V. A Sailor in the Bar Tells His Story

At noon there was a shadow by the shore
I reviewed the cloud forms and eclipses
Every odd wave and storm I'd known
Checked my left eye then my right
Slept awhile and held my head to feel for fever

I pinched my arms and legs   slapped my cheeks
Still the cold shadow was there
Seaweed was too far from shore
And fish swam through it like giraffes
Fleeing fire on the Serengeti
Then a mild dead smell in a pale green haze
Sent me back to port   shaken
Sorting memories

When I was four years old there were no rubber ducks. I loved how the soap sailed under the bridge of my skinny arm. I took Mama's string of pearls, a round box of oats, Papa's black book, one long worm and two potatoes into the tub. Took awhile for the oats and worm to sink but the rest hit bottom fast. When Mama came to check behind my ears (what ever could there have been in the small space behind my ears?) her skin turned grey. I got scared, I can't remember the words only the sound of it, of how I had ruined everything. This was just the first time I knew she hated me. After that bath I always watched, made sure her cheeks stayed pink, made sure no shadow crossed her to cross me.

Now the sailor is left alone
By the crowd of men come from the sea
They too pulled in by a hunch
Yet abandoning the past with a flinch
And after a few, feeling no fear he is left to his own words—
A sloppy drunk   tears bounce off a button
Only to puddle on his narrow lap
Mama, Mama, I cried, storm is coming
Oh hush up now boys don't cry Do you see
        Papa crying?

VI. Dear Friend, the Terror Ends

Remember when I was subject to the whims of women,
Pushed farther than any man would want to dare
Women bled me blended with me   sulked
Found new friends, haggled over details, cast the limelight
    of idle talk on my walls
No more now
No more sound of knuckles rapping glass
No more screams of the boy inside the man
    who within me now emerges
No more
I tried to raise from the ground a good mother
To swim in the jasmine stream of women
    who would gladly slash the chest cage
        feed heart to hawks   suck blood of words
Who would have to know more of me
        than one needs know of anyone
Dear Friend
You alone reside in the house of heart intact
Where I feel a bright freedom to die for
And leave behind the fear which thrills
If you call blackness of night shadow a thrill
And choose to be excited by what will destroy you.

So it happened like this—
I was in his bed   I didn't know
She was still his lover
She hurt him   he hurt her   I waited
One night she was back   in his bed
I thought this hurt me, but no!
See how the red scarf holds my hair neat
As I stand pressed to the rail of the ship
Face to the wind and weather this ocean voyage!

FORTY-THREE

After giving careful consideration
    to the needs and beliefs of others
I am inclined to spend my life
Making clay tablets of my own ideas
Mount them on the wall
Genuflect to the inner message
Rejoice that when I die
    I die alone.
Alive I may encourage another
Life or two, feel a little jazzle
If eyes light on my stone walls
then sleep a deeper death to know
    I left something behind.

which is the soil of poetry.
Last night as I trembled in your arms
You ask what will come of this.
Feeling your warmth I did not have the heart
To tell you the truth
I hinted at. 'For you
Nothing will come of it.'
But for me, even pained and jittery
I knew at least one poem would come of it.
At least one poem would spring from the soil
The deep dark dirt I keep calling love.

MY FRIEND ASKS IF I AM IN LOVE

I am the boulder lying
ancient in the field
as the glacier descended—
scraped, covered and rolled along
through ice time
left broken on the plain
when the sun next shone
        She asked me if I was in love
        And feeling about like that
        I wouldn't say yes not right off
        I felt only the great descent of time
        Upon my still kept life
I like backs he said
The expanse of skin, nothing stopping it
Like any glacier he is glad to be free
Of interruptions
        Snow and ice are warm and quiet
        I am a particle of the crust
        Love is inevitable
        I'm cool as blue smoke
        Dark as black ink
        When love rolls down
        Silent on the field
        I've been expecting you
        I say. So when she asked me
If I was in love
Feeling about like this
I wouldn't say yes
Not right off

PARADISE

Prince Rudolph came courting last evening
with burgundy plumage and fire red underbelly
He cooed and cawed quite nicely
although it did not rhyme I have no complaints
about the words themselves
or the swell feathers that rippled my skin
The dance on all sides of me was performed admirably
so at last we did relax and sleep courteously
Morning he flew to the jungles of Nicaragua
I lay speckled eggs in a paper nest and
Marvel at the thought of hatching
A strong mixed brood of spirit and earthly sense

HIS EYES

black brows over blue skies—
both of us lying
like dry timber in late July.
passion same as tension—
if the animal is not happy
the spirit stays trapped.
i'm sure of that.

INTO TOES

Neither faked nor flattered
A woman needs to be wooed
As well I think a man
With chest felt hard by chest
To spring life
Past timidity and into toes
Who curl like unborn babes
And grin and grin—
Reflection of the soul

SUNDAY AFTERNOON

I Told You I Loved You on the Rock by the Yuba

Before this is over
I want to tell you the names.
(I think you asked for more identity)
Path we walked is the Sierra Gateway Trail
Black butterfly who flew to only purple flowers,
Pipe vine swallowtail
Creamy white pink haired flower I fingered,
Early Chinese lantern.
A week earlier we might have missed
The fiddleneck curled tight, orange flowers within
We saw them opened with smooth bend.
Prickly balls bright green on the vine
Wild cucumber, big-root or man root.
A friend spent seven years saving that land
He's the one who told me the names
When I said it was Paradise there
His smile was another face of heaven
His desire more fulfilled
Than ours had ever been.

IMAGINE THE FUTURE

She asks me first if I know his past, then if I can imagine the future.
Then she just tells me. He was with that one for a year, another for two
years; nothing ever lasts with him. Why do I want to bother she asks me.
Then she tells me. You don't want to bother. Find yourself someone
reliable, someone who doesn't track every woman he meets. He's gonna
be gone soon she tells me. Then she asks me. You don't want to be left
alone at your age do you? Then she tells me I don't want to see you left
alone. I hate the thought of you alone here in this house at night. Then
she starts to ask me again. You don't want to be here every night alone,
do you?

But I can't stand it anymore. I start to wonder why does she care so I
tell her I like being alone in the house. I like watching the sun set over
the mountains and then seeing the moonlight in my bedroom window.
Sure it's nice when he's here. When he's not here, I sit out and watch the
stars.

Then she asks me as if she hadn't asked me before. You want to
spend the rest of your life sitting out alone in the dark watching the stars?

I try in my mind to figure out why she's got a thing about stars then I
say out loud, some nights I read books or just think. I like to think about
things.

But he's going to break your heart she says then she asks you want to
get your heart broken again? And then she tells me you don't want to get
your heart broken. I can't stand to feel your heart ache again.

I start imagining this broken heart. I wonder how another person
can break my heart, at least anymore than I already broke it myself ...
what could he do? I think maybe she knows so I ask her what do you
mean he'll break my heart? How will he do that?

One day you'll come home from work early and he'll be in bed with
another woman she says.

Oh no I tell her he wouldn't do a thing like that. Then I ask her why do you think he'd do something like that?

That's what men like him do, they just do she tells me, then she asks me do you want to come home to that scene?

Wait a minute, what do you mean, men like him. What do you think he's like I ask her.

He's just no good. He'll cheat on you. He never stayed with anyone. You want to be left alone? You want something like that? she asks again as if it's a question.

I told you I don't care about alone. Being alone is fine. You can visit me more, that's all. Then I wonder out loud to her what are you going to do when Frank dies?

Why are you asking me about Frank dying Frank's fine she says.

Well, he is twenty years older than you are do you think he's the one who's going to be sitting alone with the stars? Then I tell her even though I think later it wasn't very nice, I tell her you might be alone too, maybe your heart won't be broken but if you don't like the night sky why did you marry an older man?

So she tells me we fell in love but what's this got to do with you? I'm worried about you falling for a guy with no future she says to me. Then she asks me what's Frank and I got to do with it?

ACCUSATIONS

What muscle you build
as you hold that heavy flagpole
and wave your word freedom in my face!
How sad you seem in your prison,
your stupid prison of freedom!

How often I stand strong in the doorway
arms folded across a chest
puffed with the pride of truth!
How much misery lies
under my closed wings!

OFFSPRING OF A LIE

What can I say of the trembling in my blood
Or of the curse I screech to ease it
Sending waves pounding on arterial walls
Clear blood breaking over jetties through eyeballs
Vanishing into sand dunes, my cheeks,
Converging into one sharp drop,
A tension marker on the throat
Keep away from this place.
I can't talk yet.
Yet I would if I could unearth something interesting
About this anger: a narrow vein I trace back
To some other anger, digging my way in before mother and father
Before Jesus even, before pyramids and heart disease
Something before when people were only bones and teeth
In shallow graves (where they stay still tumbled in love)
Before lizards and beige seaweed
Back when anger was one cell
Fallen from the sky—an accident
Offspring of a lie
Told on another planet
Resurrection of an early martyr
Self-realized on earth.

* * * * * * * * * * * *

A stranger overhearing told me
What I had done was immoral.
(It was very small, a pinprick relative to the Holocaust)

I told him this is how I happened to see
I could kill, maybe not the body
But the feeling in the dream stage.
You should not have spoken so he insisted.
(Hadn't I already confessed? Isn't it enough to say *I know?*)
I repeated here we did not dwell in morality
This was another place: a planet carved from ice blocks
Set to drift on the dark green seas
Between continents of martyrs devoted to frostbite.
He folded and raised the newspaper from off the table
We shared by chance and sighed he was already late
He didn't say to me the pleasure had been his
Nor did I to him—pure and certain fellow
Caught in the riptide and falling hail
Of a man's blatant lie
A woman's soft and acid deception.

THE OTHER CHEEK

At the sound of a choked miaow I open the door
and a black spark with tail races off.
Good, I hope it stays away,
the mewing, the cat, any call ...

* * *

I saw until now only one face of god: the man of forgiveness
of benign smile so you want to snap your fingers
to see if he will blink—that man and that mary,
the ones on the candle glasses or nailed under your windshield wiper,
and resurrected on paper you find lying in the street
during early morning walks with a loyal dog.
You know what I mean: the pretty ones with the halos.
I raised myself on an idea of god
Culled from fairy tales and shampoo ads where every gorgeous face
Mirrors the good, kind and generous real person within
So if I wanted a prince it was simple enough
I would try for the compassion of oval mary
of the well conditioned hair encased in light.
I would need nothing for myself, now cinderella on the hearth
tirelessly radiating good-will at nerve wracking chores
now princess mary, my nose gets smaller,
my hair blacker 'til ravens get lost in the strands
my cheek lays apples, my lip rubies, my hen golden eggs.
Then the prince kisses me, I turn the other cheek
and peaches roll out of that one into a pale blue bowl
(Yes of course in my spare time I dug the clay and made the bowl)
This was the god who gave everything if I were good enough
and god dammit I was good enough. I was sure of it.

But if I were so good, I said to her, how could his lies
give way to my lies, how could his cruelty
make an excuse for my own, how could even murder
seem simple and close, and theft just a bubble blown in a loop.
What is betrayal but the result of what the other guy
craved for himself and fraud, a natural reaction
to this game world of easy credit—
And if these crimes are beyond your scope
what about the lies I tell to the dentist, why
I can't make it to a thousand different appointments
why I don't return calls, don't answer letters, forget a date.
Do you know how insane it is to be good? I asked her and she said
Inside all of us there is something terrible and dark,
something that could deceive, rob, torture, kill,
something wicked, something cruel.
And as she spoke that man and that mary turned their heads
Full circle like owls: smiles no longer closed mouth
Tidy crescent moons, now teeth showed, uppers and lowers
Lips pulled tight way beyond gum lines
Nostrils arched as if gateways to the brain
Eyes about to jump socket fixed at me and past me
Into a stew of steam like a facial from hell
which made sense
because this man and this mary had great skin also.
I'm not talking apples and peaches, this is real inner glow—
briquettes when they are best for roasting,
inside all fire when the long pale flames have stopped their pranks,
when the teens grow up you can't see it as well
but you'll get burned much worse now.
Those were the other cheeks I saw on the spin face of god.

(Do you hear the cat? she asked. No I believe
there is no cat. I can't feed another cat.
You can't just wish it away she said,
You have to decide what to do.)
But I never thought I'd have to choose
they don't advertise the other face of god,
no one said I could be stepmother, crook, stepsister or crank
the wrinkled one who kicks the kids into the stove
and sets round with skulls the chicken legged house.
Now I must decide for warts or against warts,
removal by acid or laser, which scars show least?
It was a snap to be the cold northern princess, the virgin icy
waltzing with purity in ballgown rigged up to a midnight beeper—
reminder from mother that something isn't totally real here, not yet.

                              * * *

Not a cat, it's a lost black kitten
Asleep in the sun on my roof
A paraclete sent from the backside of god.
I have had my fill of ash buckets and blue bowls
I relish the cubes of baked kid and pick at the flesh
Left dangling on the skulls of men.
I risk indigestion and this smile you see now like one on
A snake fat with weekly rat (still as an empty jar)
it's not happiness, it's lack of need.

Here kitty, kitty, kitty
This is not princess mary of the blue skies and sunny smiles.
Come on down now, don't be afraid
This is not princess mary of fading desires and peace in the face of diminishment.
That's it, a little closer now, I won't hurt you
This is not princess mary of hopeless honesty, of the lies rammed sweetly
under the cinders in your fireplace.

74

OK kitty good kitty a few more steps
This is not princess mary of the small nose growing smaller
until I can not smell at all the marvels under your arm.
Oh so you do like fish, have another bite before I take you off the roof
This is not princess mary of the 'I am doing this for you
because I do love you all' experiment in religion.
This is the kitchen, kitty, here's your dish of fish
And that's your pale blue water bowl
I made it myself in a night class for adults

* * *

The black kitten expands on my bed
In the afternoon sun when words fail me
I rest next to her. Staring into her
Copper eyes rimmed in lime I give up
Trying to be good then fall asleep deep,
Heavy into the full splendor and heat
of paradise.

TRIUMPH

On Thursday night I sat with 5 happily married women
Triumph of the imagination
I loved it like I love the silver green of early Spring.
Is Winter real—Spring, the illusion
Or is Spring fact, Winter the trick?
How can I have lasting happiness
When the rest of the world lives and dies
Over and over again?

LOVE IS NOT

Love is not what we were told
Nor what we dreamt when winter held us tight
Nor what we read, word thirsty ravens.
I am a writer and I can tell you
Love is not what writers say
Nor poets, breathing between despair and divinity.
Love is not what we were told.
Yet these nights gone from you
Feel strange as with you felt
When we first met.

OLD HAUNTS

Of course they never call
They are married now to other women now
They call those women same as they called
Me before I reached for separate
Quarters and declared myself free.
What haunts women, what ghost threads, what clear
Filament ties me to calls from men
I not only do not know now but somehow
Never knew and who never knew me shadowed
As I was and mottled under the maple tree.

WHAT LOVE

What love makes child a woman
    Where desire holds hands with soup ladles
    and fingers grey buttons on grey vests
        When thanks give way to protection
        and sex a work of one and another uncovering
        uncovering inviting revealing opening
        and crying or the flip—laughing
           What love
What love makes woman a child
    Where cradled in an older arm
        Desire melts down to infancy
        and all that is left of sex, the rocking
        rocking flicking shaking sprouting—
Long sighs pulled from a well kissed grizzled beard
Then peace, patience—dark of the rain.

THE STRANGER

He took the seat next to mine
Old red one worn by film passion
Grinding toward the springs
Married he asked No I said
Just an agreement and the stranger
Scoffed while the previews began.
Convenience then for you and him
No I said not at all like that.
Do you love him?
That question again, the darkness
But I already love you and all of them
I point into the theatre of flickering light
I love the flower rug pressed by my feet
Faded sky before I entered here
Frost forming now on every surface.
I mean, he said louder over ten second clips
Of murder and mayhem, do you say
'I love you' to each other?
The feature began, car driving across desert
Or corn fields, Northern winter, past lobster traps
Or magnolia trees or a city of electric regrets,
Face of star in rear view
Shaded, staring, never at the road ahead.
Yes, I say I love you to him.
This world is not cold, friends.
At the center our world is on fire.

TODAY

I fight parental atheism
A past generation who gave no solace
Only called our Grief a sickness and
Claimed our Joy a brutal denial
Of the General Agony we all must suffer
Until the authorities decide we have gone
Long enough. Today I want to tell you
I have gone on long enough.
Clouds do not stop the sun
Clouds frame the pervasive blue

ONCE AGAIN

There is only one knowing
We must repeat
Even knowing the repetition
We say it again
We are driven to remind ourselves
Of this absolute moment
Did I ever tell you how I knew
My mother loved me?
We know in repeating
More of the knowing
We know there is a moment
Being passed on and beyond
It was her fat cheeks when she smiled at me
There is nothing to think about
Only this steady silent song

TWO LIVES

I live two lives
One exactly like yours
The other so beautiful
I can hardly tell it in words.
Every instant the world is new
I can't keep up
When I close my eyes to dream
An old friend takes me in his arms
And says I love you.
I feel each trace of nerve and muscle
In his hug—this is not your life
This is my life
In it, I am held in arms
No one can see
Only now and then
Someone knows.

OCEAN

We find we are part of each drop
Part of a trickle travelling to a river
Some of a river sliding to the sea
To the human ocean of memory where
Twisted blood brain channels meet and merge.
We are not creating we are
Finding rivers.
Each sweet potato eaten I remember I
Cause you to remember you
Cause him to remember each sweet potato
Remembered moves a trickle down to a creek
Where granite guides on the grand tour
Stand sentinel to memory
Where we of gravity must join pools we must
Eddy together, to associate freely until
All water-minded meet, slap, crest and fall
Past unpayable statements, uncrowned identities.
Until we gather in the ocean of memory of conviction
Of memory of protest of memory of delights
Of memory of possibilities of memory.
(We are not creating, we are finding rivers.)
Nothing is impossible in the memory—we are here
To witness, to combine. We are here to condense
We are here to rise, to go up in a fury of steam
To gather in black clouds and to fall, each drop
We find we are part of a trickle
Travelling to a river and we are not creating.
We are finding rivers.

We are free to remember every protest and when
We remember each mule too stubborn to move us
Each mule so strong to pack us, each mule
Climbing mountains for us, each stubborn mule
Who crossed us, each memory of protest, each drop
Leaves us closer to the creek to the river to the ocean
We return to the ocean we become to the ocean we have found.
I will not fly into the sky: the angels are not monarchs.
The angels are all fish who scurry their fins in the cool water
And kiss each drop of the body we become.

WHEN IT IS GONE

On clear nights
Beyond my eyelids
Grandpa takes my small hand
We walk together toward the train tracks
There is no word for this
It is what has been given
So when it is gone
We are not afraid

BEDTIME PRAYER

Now I lay me down to sleep
I pray thee Lord my soul to keep
If I should die before I wake
I pray Zebra my soul to fake

Now she lays her down to sleep
She prays thee Mole her soul go deep
If she should die before she wake
She pray Crow her soul not break

Now he lays him down to sleep
He prays thee Snake his soul to creep
If he should shed beside the lake
He prays Carp his soul to bake

Now we lay us down to sleep
We pray thee Owl our souls to reap
If we cower and then we quake
We pray Squid our souls forsake

THE AUTHOR

Donna Hanelin is a writer who lives and teaches in Nevada City, California. She is inspired by human nature and daily walks alone in the woods.

THE ILLUSTRATOR

Eva Jordan is a student at San Francisco State University, presently studying at the Accademia di Belle Arti in Florence, Italy. In 1997 she received a fellowship to attend Yale University School of Art at Norfolk. Eva Jordan is Donna Hanelin's daughter.

COLOPHON

Designed by Robert E. Blesse at the Black Rock Press,
University of Nevada, Reno Library.
The type is Kinesis, a new Adobe
font, designed by Mark Jamra.
The cover was printed
letterpress.